Ron and Joyce Cave, both senior officials of the
Cambridgeshire Educational Authority,
have written and developed these
books to be read by children on their own.

A simple question is asked about each topic discussed
and is then immediately answered.

A second, more general question follows which is
designed to provoke further thinking by the child
and may require parental assistance.

The answers to these second questions
are found at the end of the book.

Designed and produced by
Aladdin Books Ltd
70 Old Compton Street · London W1
for: The Archon Press Ltd
8 Butter Market · Ipswich

Published in the U.S.A. 1982 by
Gloucester Press
730 Fifth Avenue · New York NY 10019
All rights reserved

Library of Congress Catalog
Card No. 82-81168
ISBN 531 03466 6

Printed in Belgium

WHAT ABOUT? SUBMARINES

Ron and Joyce Cave

Illustrated by
Roger Phillips, David West,
Roy Coombs and Paul Cooper

GLOUCESTER PRESS

New York · Toronto

© Aladdin Books Ltd 1982

Submarines

Submarines and submersibles are boats that can travel underwater. Most big submarines belong to the world's navies. They are used for attack or defense in war. They can fire torpedoes or even nuclear missiles. Submersibles are much smaller. They can be used for research and can also do underwater work such as repairing oil rigs. The naval submarine in the picture is driven by nuclear power, but diesel-powered submarines look very similar.

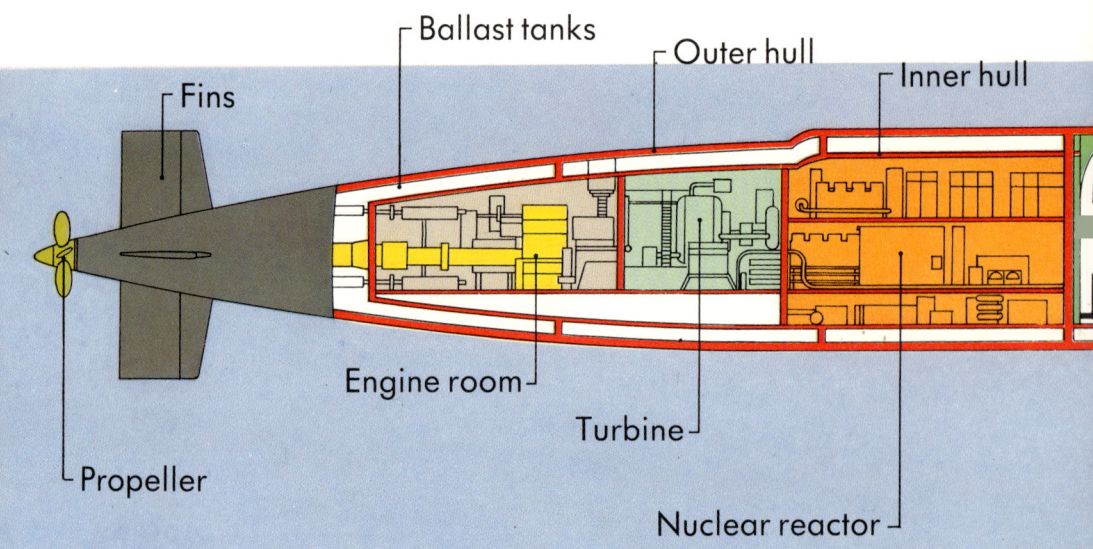

Submarines can dive deep under the sea, where the pressure of the water is very great. So their bodies, or hulls, must be very strong. Submarines are built with two hulls, one inside the other. Between the two hulls there are ballast tanks. When the tanks are full of air, the submarine floats. When water is let into the tanks, the submarine becomes heavier, and sinks underwater. The water is pumped out when the submarine wants to return to the surface.

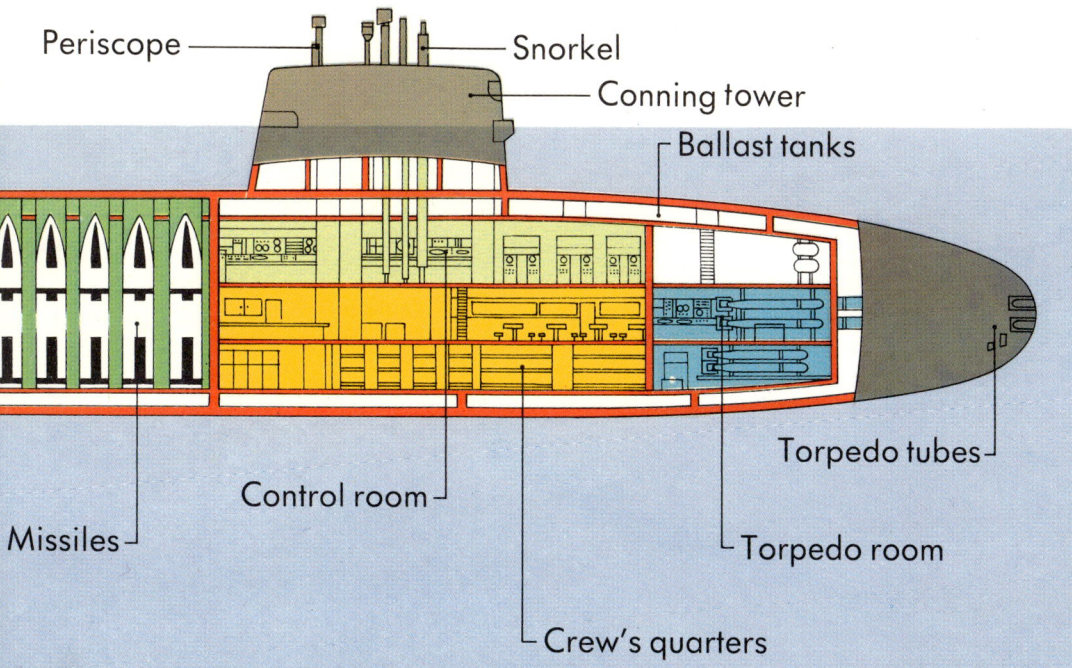

First Submarines

Just as man longed to fly, so he longed to explore the world under the sea. The first submarine to work properly was invented by a Dutchman 350 years ago. He tested it in the River Thames in London, and managed to dive to between 4 to 5 m (12 to 15 ft). King James I of England is supposed to have tried out this machine. The first submarine used in war was called the "Turtle." In 1776, during the American War of Independence, the Turtle was used to try to blow up an English ship, but the attempt failed.

How was the Turtle powered?

It was powered by a one man crew, Ezra Lee! He had to turn the propellers, or screws, by hand, work the ballast pumps, and steer. When he got to the enemy ship, he also had to drill holes in the hull and attach explosives to it. However, he failed to sink the ship.

Why do you think he failed?

The Turtle

U~Boats

Submarines were first used in large numbers during World War I (1914-18). German subs were called U-boats. Their main weapon was the torpedo. This is a self-propelled bomb, fired from tubes in the submarine. In World War II (1939-45), German subs operated in groups known as wolf packs.

How could a submarine captain tell where to aim a torpedo?

He used the periscope. This is a long tube which is raised above the sea surface. The prisms inside reflect a picture of the target back to the captain.

What does self-propelled mean?

German U-Boat

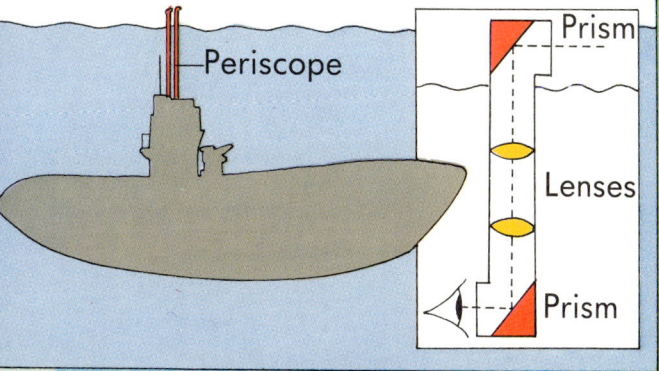

Human Torpedoes

Submarines do not only attack ships that are at sea. They can also slip into a harbor and destroy ships lying at anchor. Explosive mines, and underwater bombs called depth charges, are used to try to prevent them doing so. During World War II steel nets were hung across harbor entrances. But tiny submarines (human torpedoes) sometimes got through. Their front ends were packed with explosives that were dropped below the enemy ships.

How did the human torpedoes work?

Human torpedoes were an Italian invention. They were only 5.5 m (16 ft) long, and were driven by electric motors. Two frogmen sat astride them to steer and carry net-cutting equipment.

How are depth charges used?

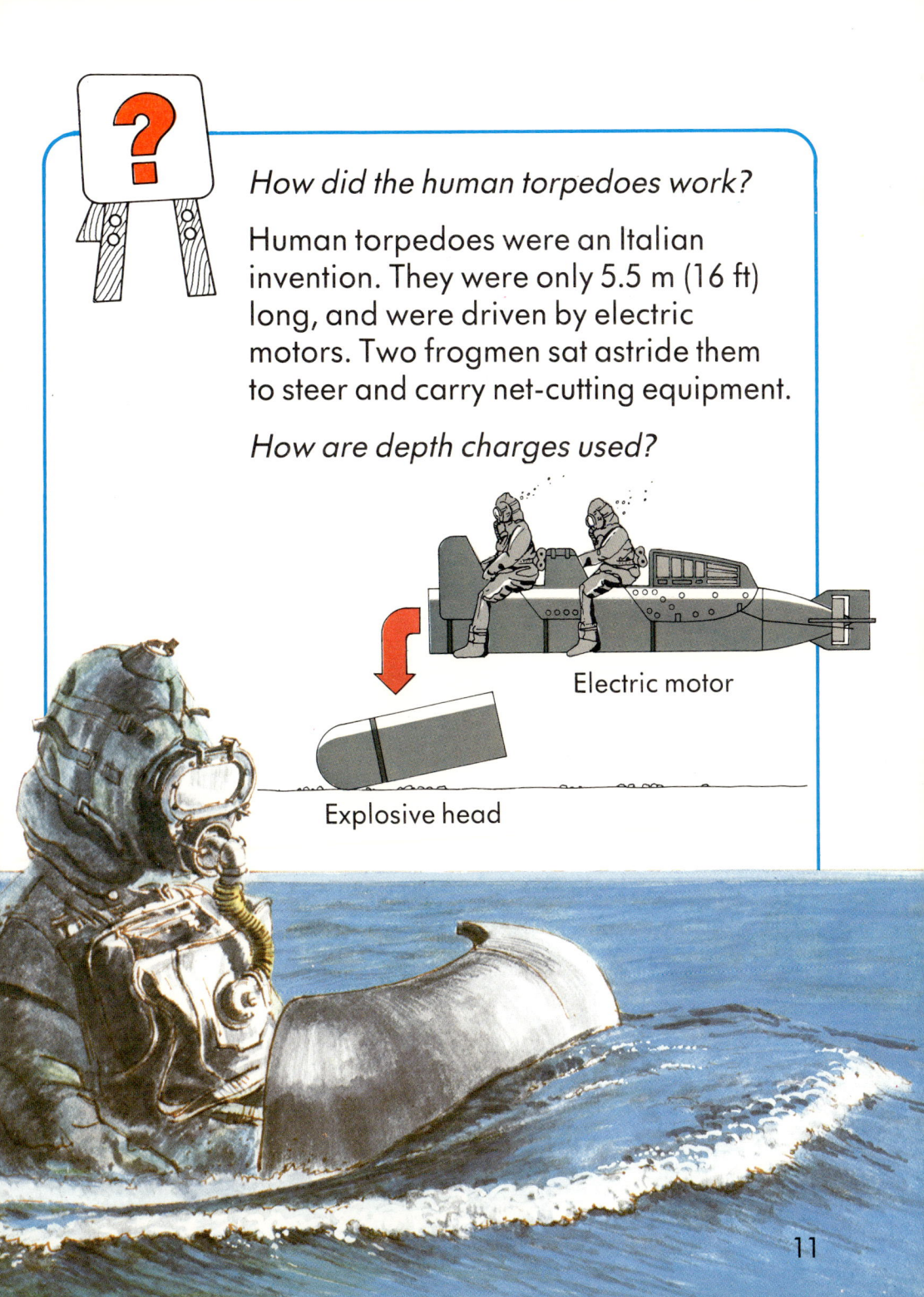

Electric motor

Explosive head

Normal Submarine

Most submarines use diesel engines and electric motors. Power comes from batteries when the sub is submerged, and from diesel engines when it is on, or just below, the surface. Diesel engines need lots of air, and can only be used when a snorkel (or breathing tube) is raised above the water. The bulge on the front of the sub shown below houses sonar equipment.

British "Porpoise" class submarine.

How is sonar equipment used?

Sonar picks up sounds underwater, such as those made by an enemy ship. Passive sonar picks up all near-by sounds. Active sonar sends out sound waves that rebound off objects. Active sonar may be heard by the enemy, so passive sonar is usually used.

Why not use radar instead?

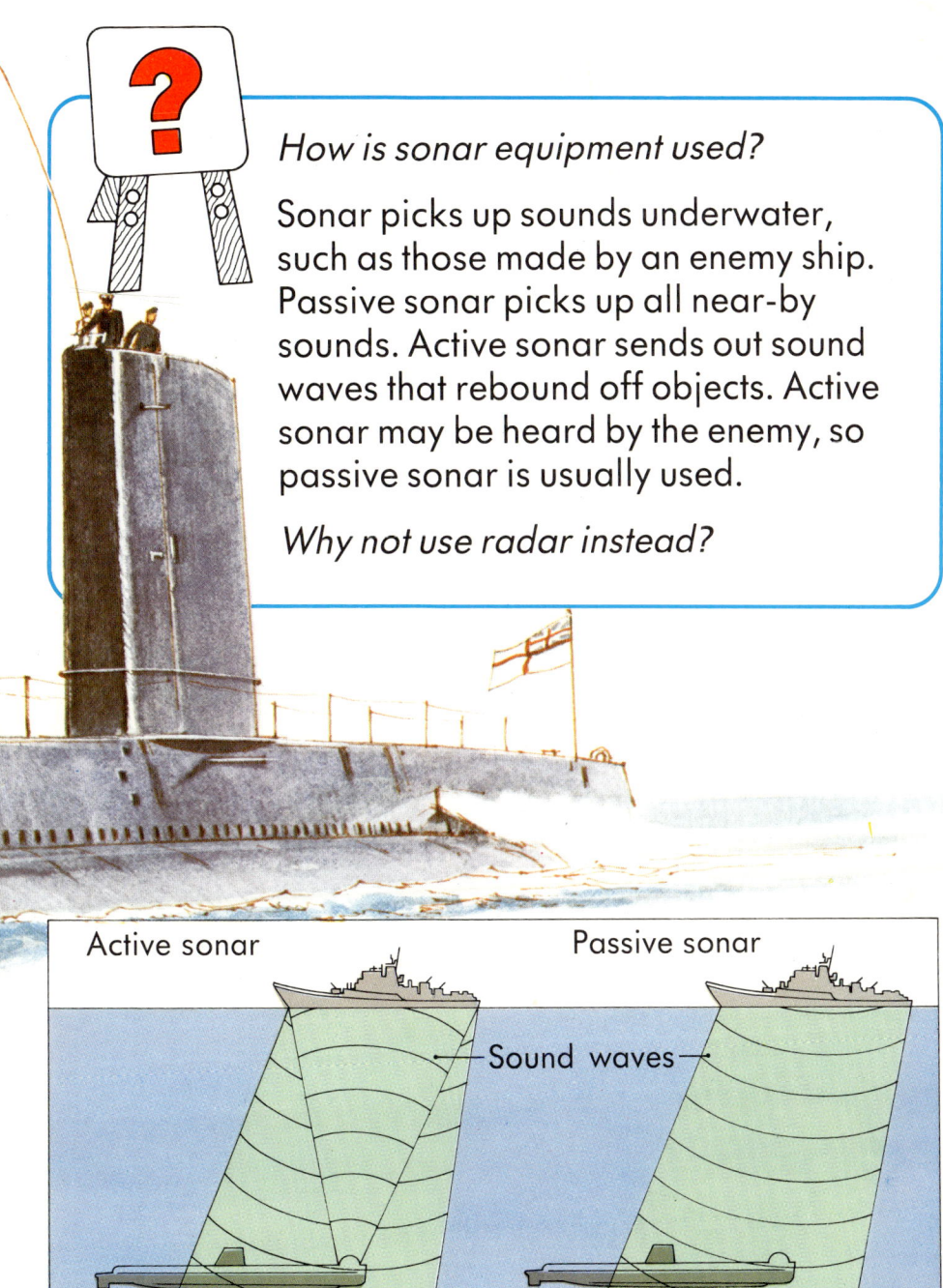

Active sonar   Passive sonar   Sound waves

Nuclear Power

Nuclear power works as well underwater as it does on land. This is how a nuclear-powered submarine works. Water is pumped around a nuclear reactor (1), to turn it into steam (2). The steam powers motors called turbines (3), that turn the propeller shaft (4). This drives the submarine through the water. The turbines also power motors called turbogenerators (5), that make electricity for the submarine.

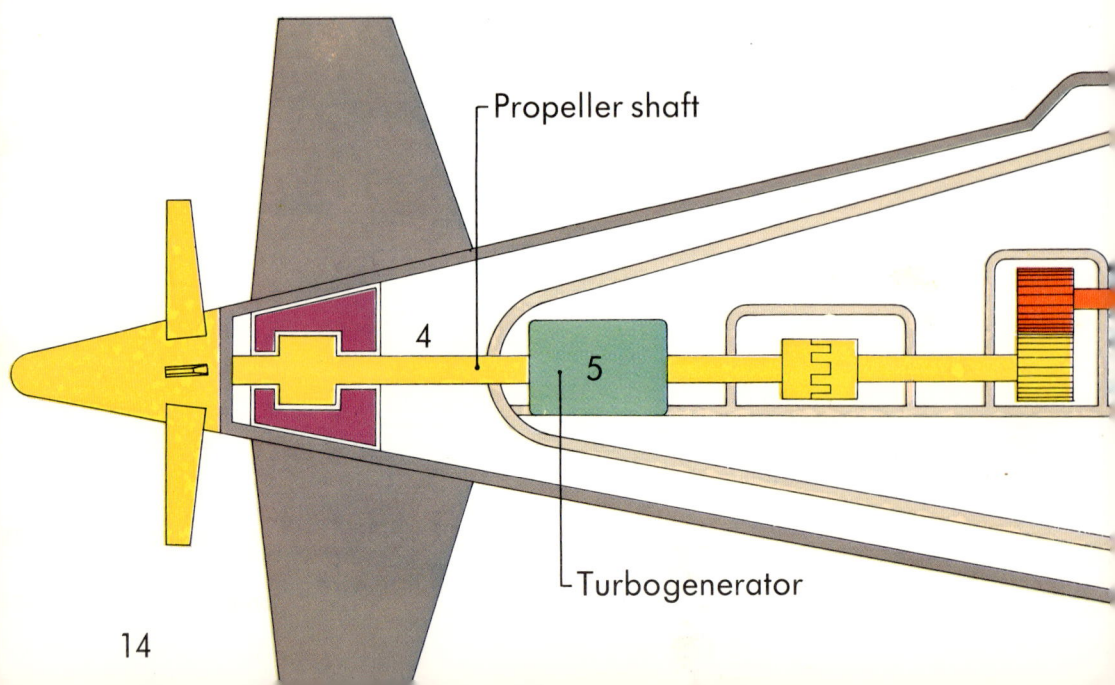

How does the reactor make the steam?

In a reactor, tiny particles called neutrons bombard atoms of uranium. The atoms split into neutrons which split more atoms. The heat energy produced by this activity turns the water to steam.

What do scientists call this process?

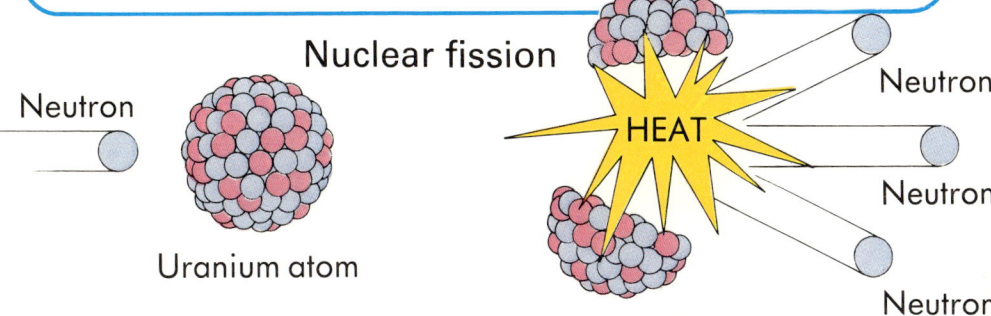

Nuclear fission

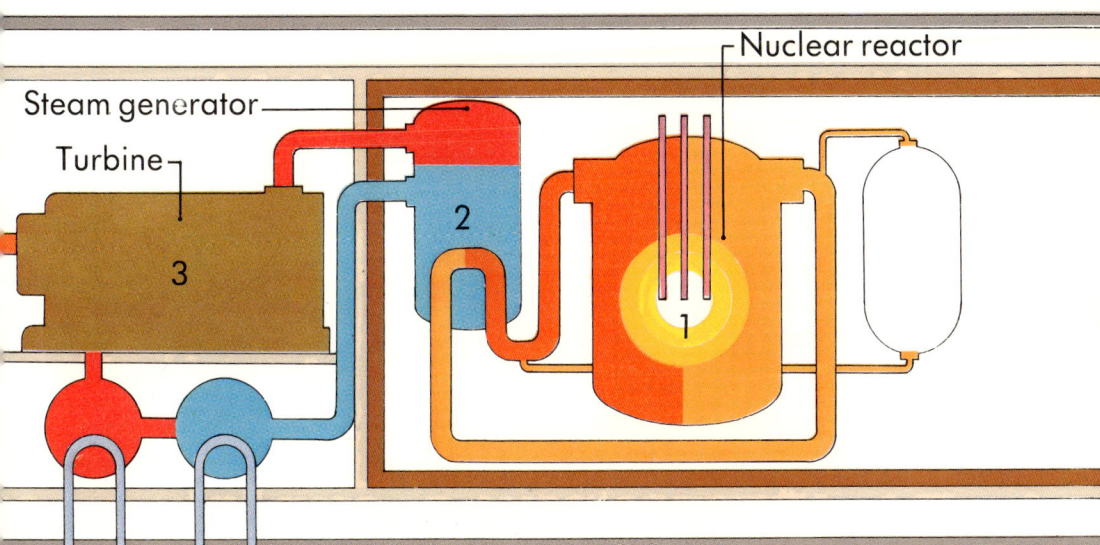

Nuclear Submarines

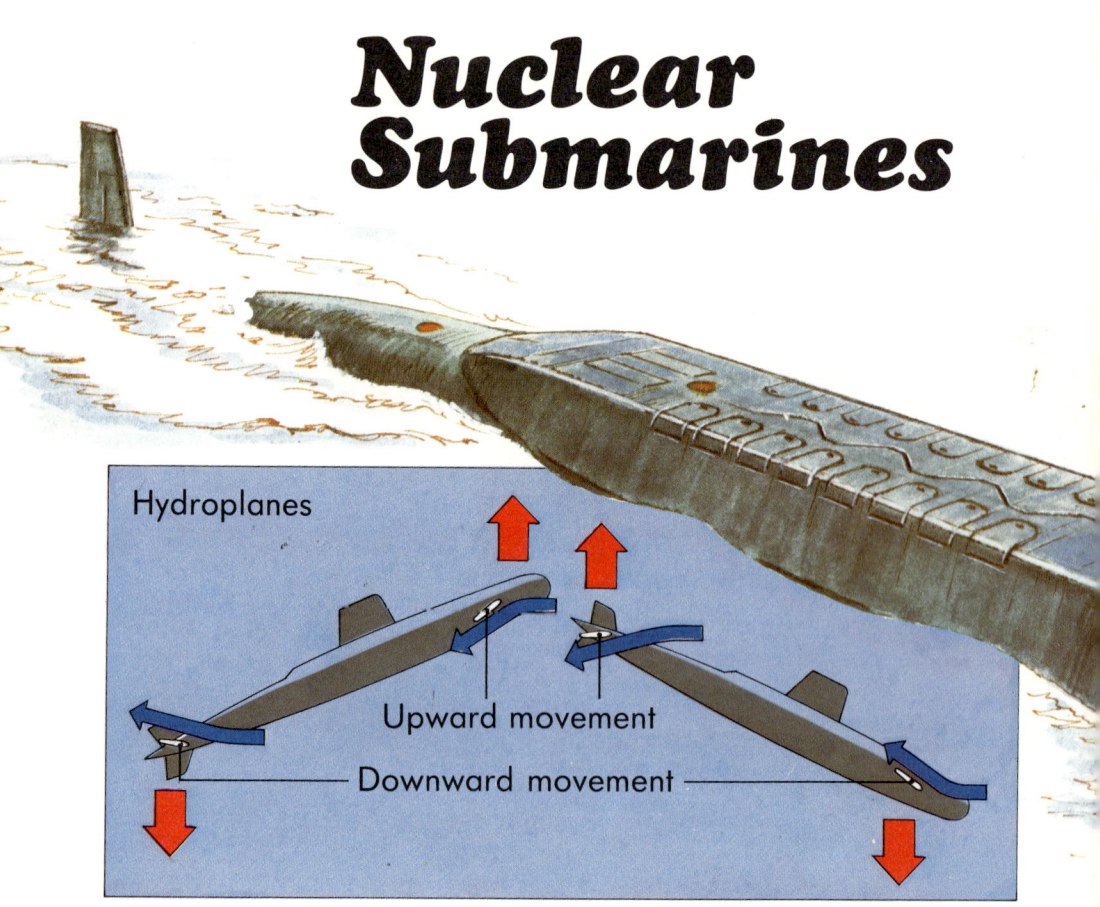

Hydroplanes
Upward movement
Downward movement

Unlike ordinary submarines, nuclear subs can stay underwater for very long periods of time. Because nuclear fuel lasts so long, they do not need to keep surfacing to refuel. A small lump of uranium is enough for a trip completely around the world! The whale-like shape of these submarines easily cuts through the water. Hydroplanes control the submarine's descent.

What are hydroplanes?

Hydroplanes are flaps on the outside of the submarine. They can be made to tilt toward or against the pressure of the water to control the movement of the sub up or down. Hydroplanes act rather like fins that help fish to move in water.

How long can nuclear subs stay underwater?

Nuclear submarine

Control Room

Directly under the conning tower lies the control room. The periscope is the eye, and the control room the brain, of the submarine. The control room is full of complicated electronic equipment. The captain in the picture is using the periscope. This is fitted with a range-finder to help him work out the distance of a target from the submarine. A navigator is working on a chart. He may be checking the submarine's position, plotting a course, or working out the details of an enemy target.

How does a navigator check his position?

Navigators used to use the position and angle of the sun or stars to check their position. Nowadays they use radio beams from space satellites. When submerged, nuclear submarines use gyroscopes. These tell a computer every change in position and speed.

What is a gyroscope?

The control room

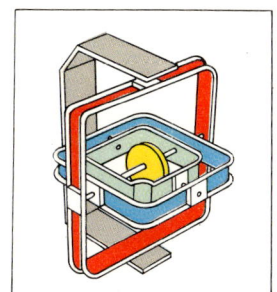

Satellite   Sun and stars   Gyroscope

Weapons

There are two main types of nuclear subs. The larger ones carry huge ballistic missiles fitted with nuclear warheads. These terrible weapons can be fired from underwater and each warhead can destroy an entire city. The giant "Ohio" submarines being built for the US Navy will carry up to 16 missiles. The missiles have a range of 9650 km (6000 miles) and can be fitted with 14 warheads. Smaller hunter/killer subs do not carry ballistic missiles, but do have other weapons.

What other weapons may be carried?

Some subs carry Cruise missiles with nuclear warheads. Ballistic missiles take only minutes to shoot into space and come back to Earth. Cruise missiles fly low, and take much longer to reach their target. Submarines also carry torpedoes and rockets that find their target by its radar pulses.

What does "ballistic" mean?

Work Underwater

Small submersibles are very useful for all kinds of underwater work. Today, many pipelines, and cables for TV and telephones, are laid under the sea, and kept in good working order, using submersibles. They are also used for salvage work and to help scientists explore the oceans. Divers cannot go as deep as submersibles unless they wear a heavy pressurized metal suit.

"Beaver IV" submersible

How does a submersible do a diver's work?

The submersible in the picture has "arms" with pincers at the ends. A man inside can use the pincers to hold tools. He can do just as well as a diver and stay down longer.

How deep can we dive without aids?

"Big Jim" diving suit

Deep Sea Explorers

The Trieste

Control room

Normal craft cannot go to the bottom of the deepest oceans. They would be crushed by the tremendous pressure. The "Trieste" is an exception. In 1960 it dived 10.9 km (6.8 miles) to the bottom of the Pacific Ocean. Tanks full of iron pellets caused it to sink. When the Trieste had to resurface, the pellets were slowly released.

Why was the Trieste not crushed?

The Trieste's hull was full of gasoline. As it dived, valves opened. The sea rushed in, squeezing the gasoline to keep it at the same pressure as the seawater itself. The hull remained intact, since the pressure on both sides of it was always the same.

How could gasoline also help the return?

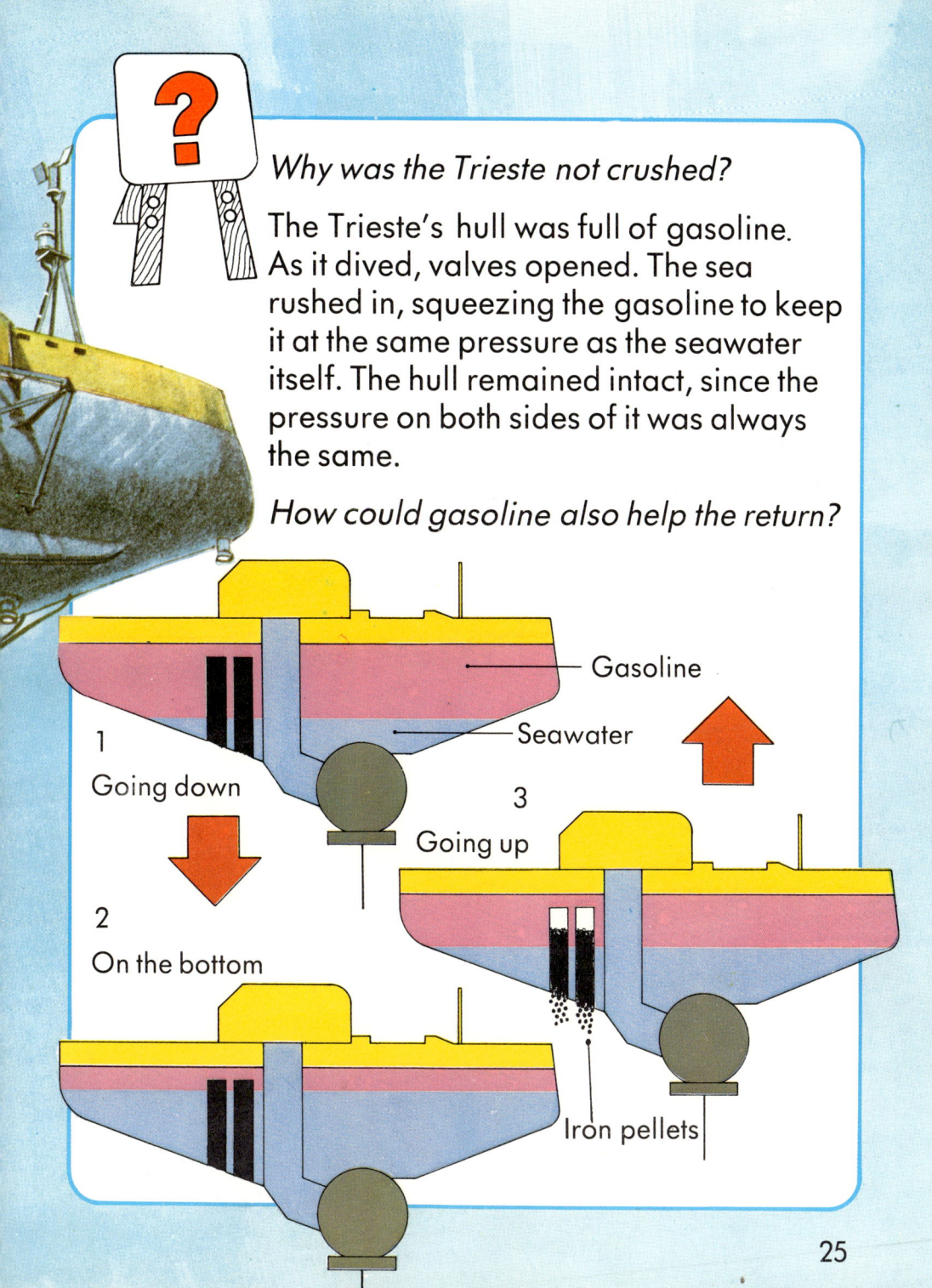

1 Going down

2 On the bottom

3 Going up

Gasoline
Seawater
Iron pellets

The Future

Exploration of the world under the sea has only just begun. In the future, all kinds of new submarines will be needed for fish farming, mining, or even for building cities under the sea. Submersibles with glass walls may be used to carry tourists underwater to see the strange fish of the ocean depths.

Underwater cargo transporter

What else may happen?

In the near future, submarine cargo ships, like the one shown below, may be built. They will be powered with nuclear reactors, so that they can travel long distances without refueling. They could travel fast in the ocean depths, avoiding bad weather on the surface. They will probably be computer-controlled.

Do you have any ideas for the future?

Answers

Why do you think he failed?

The hull of the English ship was made of metal and the Turtle's drill could not penetrate it.

What does self-propelled mean?

The torpedo has an engine of its own that drives a propeller.

How are depth charges used?

The attacking ship or plane drops the charges in a pattern around where they think the submarine is. Depth charges are set to explode at different depths.

Why not use radar instead?

Radar sends out radio pulses instead of sound waves. Radio signals can be received but not sent underwater.

What do scientists call this process?

Nuclear fission — fission means "splitting."

How long can nuclear subs stay underwater?

Nuclear subs could stay underwater for two to three years, but this would put too great a strain on the crew. In practice, dives of more than two to three weeks are uncommon.

What is a gyroscope?

You may have seen a toy gyroscope. It is a device that always stays upright, even on moving surfaces, because of a heavy wheel spinning inside it.

What does "ballistic" mean?

It means something, usually a weapon, that follows a parabolic, or curved, flight path.

How deep can we dive without aids?

The record skin dive is 85.9 m (282 ft).

How could gasoline also help the return?

Since gasoline is lighter than water, once the iron pellets had been released, the gasoline inside the Trieste made it lighter than the water around.

29

Index

ballast pumps 6
ballast tanks 4, 5
"Beaver IV" 22
"Big Jim" 23

computer 18
conning tower 5, 18
control room 5, 18, 19, 24

depth charges 10, 11, 28
diesel submarines 4, 12-13
divers 22, 23, 29

electric motors 11, 12

gyroscope 18, 19, 29

hulls 4, 5
human torpedoes 10-11
hunter/killer 20, 21
hydroplanes 16, 17

missiles 4, 5, 20, 21, 29

nuclear
 fission 28
 reactor 4, 14, 15
 submarines 4, 14-15, 16-17, 20-1, 29

"Ohio" class 20

Pacific Ocean 24
periscope 5, 9, 18
"Porpoise" class 12
pressure 5, 24, 25
propeller 4, 6
propeller shaft 14

radar 28
rockets 20

satellites 18, 19
snorkel 5, 12, 16, 17, 29
sonar 12-13

submersibles 4, 22-3, 24-5

torpedoes 4, 8, 9, 20, 28
"Trieste" 24, 25, 29
turbogenerator 14
turbines 14, 15
"Turtle" 6, 7, 28

U-boats 8
uranium 15, 16

wolf packs 8
World War II 8